J. M. GAUTHIER

Pocket Guide to the Liturgy of the Hours

Copyright © 2024 by J. M. Gauthier

All rights reserved. No part of this publication may be reproduced, stored or transmitted in any form or by any means, electronic, mechanical, photocopying, recording, scanning, or otherwise without written permission from the publisher. It is illegal to copy this book, post it to a website, or distribute it by any other means without permission.

First edition

*This book was professionally typeset on Reedsy.
Find out more at reedsy.com*

Contents

	Introduction	iv
1	Understanding the Liturgy of the Hours	1
2	Getting Started	6
3	Morning Prayer (Lauds)	15
4	Midday Prayer (Sext)	30
5	Evening Prayer (Vespers)	37
6	Night Prayer (Compline)	42
7	The Office of Readings	46
8	Conclusion	52

Introduction

The purpose of the "Pocket Guide to the Liturgy of the Hours Guide" by J. M. Gauthier is to serve as a comprehensive and accessible resource for individuals seeking a deeper understanding and engagement with the Liturgy of the Hours. This guide is crafted with the intention of providing both newcomers and seasoned practitioners with the tools and insights necessary to embrace the richness of this ancient and sacred prayer tradition.

At its core, the guide aims to demystify the Liturgy of the Hours, offering a clear and concise explanation of its historical roots, significance, and structure. For many Catholics, the Liturgy of the Hours, also known as the Divine Office, can initially appear intricate and intimidating. The guide seeks to break down these barriers, inviting readers into a profound journey of prayer and spiritual contemplation.

One fundamental aspect addressed in the guide is the historical background of the Liturgy of the Hours. By delving into its origins, the guide helps readers appreciate the evolution of this prayer practice over centuries. Understanding the roots of the Liturgy of the Hours contributes to a deeper sense of connection with the broader Christian tradition, fostering a sense of continuity with the prayers of countless believers throughout history.

Furthermore, the guide explores the intricate structure of the Liturgy of the Hours, elucidating the various components such as Morning Prayer (Lauds), Midday Prayer (Sext), Evening Prayer (Vespers), and Night Prayer (Compline). Each of these components is unpacked, guiding the reader through the sequence of psalms, canticles, readings, and intercessions that make up these daily prayers. This breakdown serves not only as a practical guide for those engaging in the Liturgy of the Hours but also as a means of emphasizing the rich tapestry of scripture and tradition woven into each prayer cycle.

The guide also underscores the importance of daily prayer in the life of a Catholic. It articulates how the Liturgy of the Hours is a unique and powerful way to sanctify each day, providing a structured rhythm that aligns with the Church's liturgical calendar. By incorporating morning, midday, and evening prayer into one's daily routine, individuals can cultivate a habit of constant communion with God, grounding their lives in a sacred rhythm that transcends the busyness of the secular world.

Moreover, the guide serves as a practical companion, offering insights on setting up a dedicated prayer space, selecting the appropriate edition of the Liturgy of the Hours, and utilizing additional tools and resources. These practical tips are designed to support individuals in establishing a conducive environment for prayer and selecting the resources that best suit their needs and preferences.

As a guide, it goes beyond the mere mechanics of the Liturgy of the Hours, extending into the realm of personal spirituality. It provides suggestions for personalizing the liturgical prayers, allowing individuals to bring their unique intentions, struggles, and joys into the sacred dialogue with God. This personalization transforms the Liturgy of the Hours from a ritualistic exercise into a deeply meaningful and intimate encounter with the Divine.

In essence, the "Pocket Guide to the Liturgy of the Hours Guide" strives to be a companion on the spiritual journey, offering guidance, inspiration, and practical assistance to individuals navigating the beautiful terrain of the Liturgy of the Hours. It is an invitation to dive into the depths of a prayer tradition that has nourished the souls of countless believers, fostering a profound connection with God and a sense of unity with the universal Church. Ultimately, the guide aspires to empower individuals to embrace the Liturgy of the Hours as a transformative and integral aspect of their daily lives, enriching their spiritual journey and deepening their relationship with the Divine.

Liturgy of the Hours

The Liturgy of the Hours, also known as the Divine Office, is a structured and daily prayer practice observed by the Catholic Church. Rooted in ancient Christian tradition, it serves as a means for individuals and communities to sanctify various moments of the day through communal prayer and meditation on sacred texts.

At its essence, the Liturgy of the Hours is a rhythmic and cyclical prayer, unfolding throughout the day and night. It is not just a personal devotion but a communal expression of the Church's prayer life. This liturgical practice encompasses various "hours" or distinct periods, each marked by specific prayers, psalms, readings, and intercessions.

The Liturgy of the Hours serves as a bridge between the sacred and the ordinary, infusing the day with moments of reflection, praise, and supplication. Its structure aligns with the natural rhythm of time, echoing the tradition of Jewish prayer observed in the Psalms and reaching back to the earliest Christian communities.

The psalms hold a central place in the Liturgy of the Hours, forming a backbone of praise, lament, and thanksgiving. Throughout the various hours, psalms are chanted or recited, providing a poetic and timeless connection to the worship practices of the Old Testament. These psalms serve as a universal language of prayer, expressing the full range of human emotions in dialogue with the divine.

In addition to psalms, the Liturgy of the Hours includes readings from Scripture, offering a systematic way to engage with the entire Bible over the course of a set period. The readings are carefully selected to align with the liturgical season, feasts, and solemnities, creating a harmony between the Church's liturgical calendar and the scriptural narrative.

The Liturgy of the Hours is not confined to monastic or clerical life; it is accessible to all members of the Church, inviting them to participate in the daily prayer of the Church. While traditionally associated with clergy and religious orders, the Second Vatican Council encouraged the laity to embrace this form of prayer, emphasizing its universal significance for the entire Body of Christ.

One of the distinctive features of the Liturgy of the Hours is its ability to sanctify time, transforming the ordinary moments of the day into opportunities for encounter with the sacred. By participating in this communal prayer, individuals connect with the global Church, forming a spiritual unity that transcends geographical and cultural boundaries.

In essence, the Liturgy of the Hours is a tapestry of prayer woven into the fabric of daily life, providing a framework for spiritual discipline, community engagement, and deepening one's relationship with God. It stands as a testament to the enduring vitality of ancient Christian practices, continually renewing the spiritual life of individuals and the Church as a whole.

1

Understanding the Liturgy of the Hours

The historical background of the Liturgy of the Hours is deeply rooted in the early Christian practices of communal prayer and the Jewish tradition of regular prayer throughout the day. In the early centuries of Christianity, believers gathered for common prayer, and this communal aspect gradually evolved into a more formalized structure, laying the foundation for what we now know as the Liturgy of the Hours.

The roots of the Liturgy of the Hours can be traced back to the Jewish custom of praying at specific hours, known as the "Hours of Prayer." This practice is evident in the Psalms, where the psalmist expresses a commitment to praising God at various times during the day and night. Early Christians, steeped in this tradition, continued the practice of regular prayer, adapting it to reflect the new covenant in Christ.

The monastic communities of the early Church played a significant role in shaping the Liturgy of the Hours. Monks, seeking a disciplined and contemplative life, established regular patterns of prayer throughout the day. The Rule of St. Benedict, written in the 6th century, formalized these practices, prescribing specific times for communal prayer, readings, and work. The Benedictine monastic tradition profoundly influenced the development and spread of the Liturgy of the Hours throughout the Christian world.

Over the centuries, the structure of the Liturgy of the Hours continued to evolve. The breviary, a compilation of psalms, prayers, and readings organized for daily prayer, gradually took shape. By the Middle Ages, the Liturgy of the Hours became an integral part of the Roman Catholic Church's liturgical life. Popes, clergy, and religious orders embraced the practice, contributing to its refinement and dissemination.

The Council of Trent in the 16th century standardized the breviary, establishing a more uniform structure for the Liturgy of the Hours. This standardization aimed to ensure consistency across the diverse regions of the Catholic Church. The revisions made during this period laid the groundwork for the breviary used in the Roman Catholic Church today.

The Second Vatican Council in the 20th century brought significant reforms to the Liturgy of the Hours. The council emphasized the importance of active participation by the laity and encouraged a broader accessibility to this form of prayer. As a result, translations of the Liturgy of the Hours in vernacular languages became more widespread, making it accessible to a global audience.

In recent times, the Liturgy of the Hours continues to be a

vital part of the Catholic Church's liturgical tradition. Various editions and adaptations cater to the diverse needs of individuals and communities, ensuring its continued relevance in the contemporary context. The historical journey of the Liturgy of the Hours reflects the dynamic interplay between tradition, communal practice, and the spiritual evolution of the Church through the ages.

Structure of the Liturgy

The structure of the Liturgy of the Hours is a carefully organized framework that guides the praying community through distinct periods of the day, fostering a rhythm of prayer that sanctifies time. This liturgical practice, deeply embedded in the Catholic tradition, is characterized by its cyclical nature and incorporates a rich tapestry of psalms, readings, and prayers.

Morning Prayer (Lauds) marks the beginning of the liturgical day. It is a prayer of praise and thanksgiving, setting a tone of joy and gratitude as the community gathers to consecrate the day to God. Morning Prayer typically includes psalms, a canticle, readings, and intercessions.

Midday Prayer (Sext) punctuates the day, providing a moment for reflection and spiritual renewal. It acknowledges God's presence in the midst of daily activities, inviting the praying community to pause and realign their focus. Midday Prayer includes psalms, a short reading, and intercessions.

Evening Prayer (Vespers) serves as a transition from the activities of the day to the evening hours. It is a prayer of illumination, seeking God's light and guidance as the day draws to a close. Evening Prayer incorporates psalms, a canticle, readings, and intercessions.

Night Prayer (Compline) is the final prayer before retiring for the night. It embraces a spirit of surrender and trust, acknowledging God's protection during the night hours. Night Prayer typically includes psalms, a short reading, and a hymn, fostering a sense of peace and security.

The Office of Readings is a distinctive hour that can be prayed at any time of the day. It offers a more extended period of reflection, featuring additional readings from Scripture, patristic writings, or other spiritual texts. The Office of Readings allows for a deeper engagement with the Word of God and the wisdom of the Church Fathers.

Throughout the Liturgy of the Hours, the recitation of psalms holds a central place. The psalms, composed by various biblical authors, express a wide range of emotions and themes, serving as a universal language of prayer. Additionally, each hour often includes readings from Scripture, providing a structured and systematic approach to encountering the entirety of the Bible over a set period.

The Liturgy of the Hours also adapts to the liturgical calendar, incorporating special prayers, antiphons, and readings to align with the seasons and feasts of the Church. This adaptive quality ensures that the structure of the liturgy remains dynamic and responsive to the changing rhythms of the liturgical year.

In essence, the structure of the Liturgy of the Hours is a finely woven tapestry of prayer that invites the praying community to engage with the sacred at different moments of the day. This cyclical and structured approach serves not only as a form of communal worship but also as a spiritual discipline, anchoring individuals in a rhythm of prayer that transcends the ordinary and sanctifies the passing hours of each day.

2

Getting Started

The importance of daily prayer is deeply ingrained in various religious traditions and holds significant spiritual, emotional, and psychological benefits. For many, daily prayer is not merely a ritual but a profound practice that fosters a sense of connection with the divine, cultivates inner peace, and shapes one's perspective on life.

1. Communion with the Divine:
Daily prayer serves as a means of establishing and nurturing a personal relationship with a higher power, whether it be God, the Divine, or a spiritual force. It provides an avenue for individuals to express gratitude, seek guidance, and connect with the transcendent aspects of life.

2. Spiritual Grounding:
Regular prayer acts as a spiritual anchor, grounding individuals in their faith and values. It serves as a constant reminder of the sacred amidst the challenges and distractions of daily life, helping individuals stay centered and aligned with their

spiritual principles.

3. Source of Strength and Comfort:

Engaging in daily prayer can offer solace during difficult times. It becomes a source of strength, providing comfort and reassurance in the face of adversity. The act of turning to prayer in moments of struggle allows individuals to draw upon a higher power for support and resilience.

4. Reflection and Mindfulness:

Daily prayer encourages self-reflection and mindfulness. Taking time each day to pause, reflect, and engage in prayer fosters a heightened awareness of one's thoughts, actions, and emotions. This introspective practice contributes to personal growth and a deeper understanding of oneself.

5. Gratitude and Appreciation:

Prayer often involves expressions of gratitude and appreciation for the blessings in one's life. Cultivating a thankful heart through daily prayer helps individuals focus on the positive aspects of their experiences, fostering a sense of contentment and humility.

6. Moral and Ethical Guidance:

Many religious prayers include moral and ethical teachings. Engaging in daily prayer can serve as a guide for ethical decision-making, encouraging individuals to align their actions with their values and principles. It provides a moral compass in navigating life's complexities.

7. Community and Unity:

Daily prayer is not only an individual practice but can also be a communal one. Participating in group prayers fosters a sense of community and shared purpose. It reinforces a collective commitment to spiritual growth and provides mutual support within religious communities.

8. Stress Reduction and Emotional Well-being:

Studies have shown that regular prayer is associated with reduced stress levels and improved emotional well-being. The meditative and contemplative aspects of prayer contribute to a sense of calm, peace, and emotional balance.

9. Sense of Purpose and Direction:

Prayer often involves seeking guidance and purpose in life. Daily prayer helps individuals clarify their values, goals, and aspirations. It can provide a sense of direction, purpose, and a connection to a higher meaning in the midst of life's challenges.

10. Integration of Faith into Daily Life:

By incorporating daily prayer into their routines, individuals integrate their faith into the fabric of their daily lives. This integration fosters a holistic approach to spirituality, where one's beliefs permeate various aspects of life, influencing decisions, relationships, and overall well-being.

In summary, the importance of daily prayer extends beyond religious rituals; it encompasses a holistic approach to spirituality, promoting connection, mindfulness, and personal growth. Whether seeking divine guidance, solace in challenging times, or a deeper understanding of oneself, daily prayer remains a transformative practice with far-reaching benefits for individuals on their spiritual journey.

Setting up a prayer space

Setting up a prayer space is a meaningful and intentional practice that creates a conducive environment for contemplation, meditation, and spiritual connection. Here are some considerations for setting up a prayer space:

1. Choose a Quiet and Distraction-Free Area:

Select a space in your home that is quiet and away from distractions. This could be a corner of a room, a cozy nook, or even a dedicated room if possible. Minimize external disturbances to create an atmosphere of tranquility.

2. Use Natural Light and Colors:

If possible, position your prayer space near a window or utilize natural light sources. Natural light can enhance the ambiance of the space. Consider using calming and spiritually significant colors for decor to create a visually soothing environment.

3. Incorporate Symbols and Icons:

Include symbols, icons, or religious artifacts that hold personal significance. These could be religious statues, images, or symbols that represent your faith and provide a focal point for reflection during prayer.

4. Arrange Comfortable Seating:

Choose comfortable seating or cushions for your prayer space. Whether it's a chair, meditation cushion, or a prayer bench, ensure it promotes good posture and comfort for an extended period of contemplation.

5. Include Inspirational Texts:

Place sacred texts or scriptures that are meaningful to you in the prayer space. This could include your religious book, prayer books, or inspirational readings that you may want to refer to during your prayer or meditation.

6. Set Up Candle(s) or Incense:

Candles and incense can contribute to the sensory experience of your prayer space. They symbolize light, purity, and spirituality. Ensure safety by using flameless candles if necessary, and choose scents that enhance a sense of peace and focus.

7. Personalize with Meaningful Objects:

Add personal touches to your prayer space with items that hold sentimental value or evoke positive memories. This could be a piece of art, a family heirloom, or objects from your spiritual journey.

8. Create a Prayer Mat or Rug:

If you have the space, consider placing a prayer mat or rug. This helps define the sacred space and can be a symbolic gesture, signifying the separation of your prayer space from the everyday world.

9. Maintain Cleanliness:

Keep the prayer space tidy and clutter-free. Regular cleaning and organization contribute to a sense of reverence and make the space inviting for daily use.

10. Establish a Ritual:

Develop a simple ritual to mark the beginning and end of

your prayer time. This could include lighting a candle, saying a specific prayer, or engaging in a brief moment of silence. Establishing a ritual helps signal the transition into a sacred space.

11. Consider Background Music:

Soft and instrumental music can enhance the ambiance of your prayer space. Choose music that aligns with your spiritual preferences and helps create a serene atmosphere.

12. Create a Symbolic Altar:

If space permits, set up a small altar with elements that hold spiritual significance. This could include stones, flowers, or symbolic objects representing elements of your faith.

Remember that the most important aspect of setting up a prayer space is personalization. Tailor it to align with your beliefs, preferences, and the type of prayer or meditation you practice. Regularly revisiting and refreshing your prayer space can further deepen its impact on your spiritual journey.

Choosing the appropriate edition for your prayer needs is a thoughtful process that involves considering factors such as personal preferences, the specific liturgical tradition you follow, and the depth of content you desire. Here are some considerations for selecting the appropriate edition for your prayer and worship:

1. Liturgical Tradition:

Determine which liturgical tradition aligns with your spiritual practice. Different Christian denominations may have variations in the structure and content of the Liturgy of the

Hours. Ensure that the edition you choose is consistent with the liturgical practices of your faith community.

2. Translation and Language:

Consider the language of the edition. Choose a translation that resonates with you and facilitates a meaningful connection with the prayers. Some editions offer translations in the original Latin, while others provide translations in the vernacular language, allowing for a deeper understanding of the texts.

3. Comprehensive or Simplified Versions:

Decide whether you prefer a comprehensive edition that includes the complete Liturgy of the Hours with all the hours and readings, or if you would prefer a simplified version that focuses on specific hours or a condensed form. Comprehensive editions may be more suitable for those seeking a complete prayer experience, while simplified versions can be accessible for beginners or those with time constraints.

4. Single or Multi-Volume Sets:

The Liturgy of the Hours is often available in either a single-volume or multi-volume set. Single-volume editions provide the entire liturgical cycle in one book, offering convenience for daily use. Multi-volume sets may be more extensive but allow for a more detailed exploration of the texts and readings.

5. Seasonal or Year-Round Editions:

Some editions are tailored to specific liturgical seasons, such as Advent, Lent, or Easter. These seasonal editions provide focused prayers and readings relevant to the particular liturgical period. Alternatively, year-round editions encompass the complete liturgical calendar, offering prayers for all seasons and feast days.

6. Print or Digital Format:

Consider whether you prefer a traditional print edition or a digital format. Print editions provide a tangible and tactile experience, while digital versions may offer portability and additional features, such as search functionalities, bookmarking, and accessibility options.

7. Commentaries and Additional Content:

Some editions include commentaries, reflections, or additional content that provide insights into the prayers and readings. If you appreciate guidance and commentary to deepen your understanding, look for editions that offer these supplemental features.

8. Accessibility:

Ensure that the selected edition is accessible for your daily use. Consider factors such as size, font, and layout. A user-friendly format contributes to a seamless and enjoyable prayer experience.

9. Personal Recommendations:

Seek recommendations from spiritual mentors, clergy, or fellow worshippers who may have experience with specific editions. Personal testimonials can provide valuable insights into the practicality and effectiveness of a particular edition.

10. Cost and Affordability:

Consider your budget when selecting an edition. Different

editions may vary in price based on factors such as content, binding, and additional features. Choose an edition that aligns with your financial considerations.

Ultimately, the appropriate edition is one that resonates with your personal preferences, aligns with your liturgical tradition, and enhances your experience of the Liturgy of the Hours. Take the time to explore different editions, perhaps starting with one that aligns with your current needs and adapting as your prayer practice evolves.

3

Morning Prayer (Lauds)

Morning Prayer, also known as Lauds, is a sacred and uplifting liturgical practice that marks the beginning of the day in the tradition of the Liturgy of the Hours. This prayerful ritual invites individuals to awaken their spirits, express gratitude, and consecrate the day to God through a structured sequence of psalms, readings, and intercessions.

As the sun rises and dispels the darkness, Morning Prayer serves as a symbolic opening of the day's journey. It is a moment to acknowledge the gift of a new day and to recognize the presence of the Divine in the unfolding hours ahead. Morning Prayer, while deeply rooted in Christian tradition, transcends denominational boundaries, offering a universal call to praise, thanksgiving, and spiritual alignment.

Structure of Morning Prayer:

Opening Invocations:
 Morning Prayer often begins with an opening verse or an-

tiphon that sets the tone for the prayer. This may be followed by an invitation to prayer, invoking the presence of the Holy Spirit.

Hymn:

A hymn is sung or recited, serving as a lyrical expression of praise and worship. The choice of hymn may vary based on liturgical seasons or personal preference.

Psalmody:

The heart of Morning Prayer lies in the chanting or recitation of psalms. These sacred songs, attributed to various biblical authors, encompass themes of praise, gratitude, and trust. Typically, three psalms are included, interspersed with antiphons that emphasize key verses.

Canticle:

A canticle from the New Testament, often the Benedictus (the Song of Zechariah), is recited. This canticle is a proclamation of God's salvation and mercy, connecting the Old and New Testaments in the morning liturgy.

Scripture Reading:

A short passage from the Bible is read, providing additional scriptural insights and reflections. The reading is chosen to complement the themes of the psalms and canticle.

Responsory:

A responsory or short response is recited, often connecting the scripture reading to the themes of the psalms and emphasizing a communal response to God's Word.

Benedictus Es, Domine:

This brief acclamation, meaning "Blessed are You, O Lord," is often included, underscoring the praise and adoration offered to God during Morning Prayer.

Intercessions:

The prayer of intercession follows, where the community lifts up intentions for the Church, the world, and individuals. This section invites active participation, fostering a sense of unity and concern for others.

Lord's Prayer:

Morning Prayer typically includes the recitation of the Lord's Prayer, a unifying prayer shared by Christians worldwide.

Concluding Prayer:

The liturgy concludes with a prayer that sums up the themes of Morning Prayer and asks for God's blessings for the day ahead.

Morning Prayer, in its entirety, encapsulates a holistic approach to worship, weaving together the beauty of psalms, the richness of scripture, and the communal spirit of intercession. It serves as a spiritual foundation for the day, guiding individuals to align their hearts with divine grace, purpose, and thanksgiving as they embark on the journey ahead.

Below is a guide to Pray the Morning Prayer

Opening Invocations

The opening invocations in Morning Prayer set the tone for the sacred encounter, inviting individuals to enter into a spirit of reverence and communion with the Divine. These invocations serve as a contemplative bridge, signaling the beginning of the prayerful journey and inviting the presence of the Holy Spirit. While specific invocations may vary based on liturgical traditions, here's a general representation:

Leader (L): In the name of the Father, and of the Son, and of the Holy Spirit.

All (A): Amen.

L: O God, come to our assistance.

A: Lord, make haste to help us.

L: Glory to the Father, and to the Son, and to the Holy Spirit.

A: As it was in the beginning, is now, and will be forever. Amen.

These opening invocations establish a sacred rhythm, aligning the praying community in a shared declaration of faith and dependence on the Divine. The call upon the Holy Trinity—the Father, the Son, and the Holy Spirit—acknowledges the Triune Godhead and invokes the presence of the Divine in the act of worship.

The subsequent plea for assistance and hastening of the Lord's help acknowledges human frailty and the need for divine intervention. It echoes the sentiments expressed in various psalms, where the psalmist seeks God's prompt assistance and mercy in times of need.

The final declaration of glory emphasizes the timeless nature of God, recognizing His eternal existence and majesty. The refrain, "As it was in the beginning, is now, and will be forever," underscores the perpetual praise and adoration offered to God throughout time.

This opening sequence of invocations not only establishes a framework for the prayer but also invites participants to enter into a collective space of worship and surrender. It reflects a timeless tradition, connecting the contemporary praying community with the countless believers who, through the ages, have begun their daily prayers with similar invocations, fostering a sense of continuity in the tapestry of faith.

Psalmody

Psalmody holds a central place in the Liturgy of the Hours, including Morning Prayer. These sacred songs, attributed to various biblical authors, are a poetic expression of praise, thanksgiving, lament, and trust. The recitation or chanting of psalms during Morning Prayer forms a rhythmic and contemplative sequence, allowing the praying community to engage with the rich tapestry of emotions and themes encapsulated in these timeless verses.

Morning Prayer typically includes a set of three psalms, chosen to resonate with the liturgical season, feast day, or thematic focus. Here's a representation of how psalmody is structured during Morning Prayer:

Psalm 95: A Call to Worship and Thanksgiving

Antiphon: O come, let us worship the Lord, singing joyfully to God our Savior.

Psalm 95:

Verses 1-2: O come, let us sing joyfully to the Lord; let us acclaim the rock of our salvation.
Verses 3-5: Let us come into his presence with thanksgiving;

let us joyfully sing psalms to him.

Verses 6-7: Come, let us bow down in worship; let us kneel before the Lord who made us.

Antiphon: O come, let us worship the Lord, singing joyfully to God our Savior.

Psalm 100: A Hymn of Praise and Thanksgiving

Antiphon: Cry out with joy to the Lord, all the earth. Serve the Lord with gladness.

Psalm 100:

Verses 1-2: Cry out with joy to the Lord, all the earth; serve the Lord with gladness.

Verses 3-4: Know that the Lord is God, he made us, we belong to him, we are his people.

Verse 5: Go within his gates, giving thanks; enter his courts with songs of praise.

Antiphon: Cry out with joy to the Lord, all the earth. Serve the Lord with gladness.

Psalm 67: A Prayer for God's Blessings

Antiphon: Let the peoples praise you, O God; let all the peoples praise you.

Psalm 67:

Verses 1-2: O God, be gracious and bless us; let your face shed its light upon us.

Verses 3-4: So will your ways be known upon earth and all nations learn your saving help.

Verses 5-6: Let the nations be glad and exult, for you rule the world with justice.

Antiphon: Let the peoples praise you, O God; let all the peoples praise you.

The antiphons serve as refrains that punctuate the psalms, emphasizing key themes and fostering a sense of unity in the community's prayer. The selection of psalms during Morning Prayer varies each day, providing a diverse and rich experience of engaging with the entirety of the Psalter over the liturgical cycle. Psalmody in Morning Prayer, with its blend of ancient wisdom and contemporary relevance, invites participants into a sacred dialogue with God and the community of believers across time.

Canticle

A canticle in the context of Morning Prayer is a hymn or song, often taken from the New Testament, that serves as a joyful proclamation of God's salvation and mercy. The choice of a specific canticle varies depending on the liturgical day and season. One of the most commonly used canticles during Morning Prayer is the "Benedictus," also known as the Song of Zechariah, which is found in the Gospel of Luke (Luke 1:68-79).

Canticle: The Benedictus (Song of Zechariah)

Leader (L): Blessed be the Lord, the God of Israel; he has come to his people and set them free.

All (A): He has raised up for us a mighty Savior, born of the house of his servant David.

L: Through his holy prophets he promised of old that he would save us from our enemies, from the hands of all who hate us.

A: He promised to show mercy to our fathers and to remember his holy covenant.

L: This was the oath he swore to our father Abraham: to set us free from the hands of our enemies.

A: Free to worship him without fear, holy and righteous in his sight all the days of our life.

L: You, my child, shall be called the prophet of the Most High; for you will go before the Lord to prepare his way.

A: To give his people knowledge of salvation by the forgiveness of their sins.

L: In the tender compassion of our God, the dawn from on high shall break upon us.

A: To shine on those who dwell in darkness and the shadow of death, and to guide our feet into the way of peace.

L: Glory to the Father, and to the Son, and to the Holy Spirit.

A: As it was in the beginning, is now, and will be forever. Amen.

The "Benedictus" is a song of praise and expectation, attributed to Zechariah, the father of John the Baptist. It celebrates the coming of the Messiah, recognizing the fulfillment of God's promises and the dawn of salvation. This canticle is a poignant expression of hope, acknowledging the role of John the Baptist in preparing the way for Jesus and highlighting the mercy and compassion of God.

Canticles like the "Benedictus" in Morning Prayer serve as moments of heightened praise and reflection, adding a distinctive musical and lyrical quality to the rhythm of the liturgy. They enrich the worship experience by incorporating the voices of biblical figures into the communal prayer, connecting the praying community with the prophetic anticipation of God's redemptive work.

Scripture Reading

In Morning Prayer, a scripture reading is included to provide additional insights and reflections on the themes of the day. The chosen reading often complements the psalms, canticle, and liturgical season. Here is a representation of how a scripture reading might be structured during Morning Prayer:

Leader (L): A reading from the Letter of St. Paul to the Ephesians.

All (A): Blessed be the God and Father of our Lord Jesus Christ, who has blessed us in Christ with every spiritual blessing in the heavenly places.

L: He chose us in Christ before the foundation of the world to be holy and blameless before him in love.

A: He destined us for adoption as his children through Jesus Christ, according to the good pleasure of his will.

L: In him we have redemption through his blood, the forgiveness of our trespasses, according to the riches of his grace.

A: This grace he lavished upon us, with all wisdom and insight.

L: He has made known to us the mystery of his will, according to his good pleasure that he set forth in Christ.

A: As a plan for the fullness of time, to gather up all things in him, things in heaven and things on earth.

L: In Christ, we have also obtained an inheritance, having been destined according to the purpose of him who accomplishes all things according to his counsel and will.

A: So that we, who were the first to set our hope on Christ, might live for the praise of his glory.

L: In him, you also, when you had heard the word of truth, the gospel of your salvation, and had believed in him, were marked with the seal of the promised Holy Spirit.

A: This is the pledge of our inheritance toward redemption as God's own people, to the praise of his glory.

L: The word of the Lord.

A: Thanks be to God.

This scripture reading is an excerpt from the Letter to the Ephesians, offering insights into the spiritual blessings, adoption as children of God, redemption through Christ's sacrifice, and the role of the Holy Spirit. It serves as a moment of reflection and meditation, deepening the connection between the psalms, canticle, and the broader biblical narrative. The responsive "Thanks be to God" acknowledges the richness of the Word and expresses gratitude for the scripture reading shared within the community of believers.

Responsory

The responsory in Morning Prayer is a short, often antiphonal, response that follows the scripture reading. It typically connects the themes of the reading to the psalms and serves as a collective affirmation or prayerful response. Here's a representation of how a responsory might be structured:

Leader (L): The Word of the Lord.

All (A): Thanks be to God.

L: In the tender compassion of our God,

A: The dawn from on high shall break upon us.

L: To shine on those who dwell in darkness and the shadow of death,

A: And to guide our feet into the way of peace.

In this responsory, the words echo themes from the scripture reading, emphasizing the tender compassion of God and the dawning of divine light to guide people out of darkness. It creates a rhythm of call and response, fostering a sense of unity in the community's prayer and reinforcing the spiritual insights gained from the preceding scripture reading. The responsory serves as a moment of contemplation and proclamation, linking the Word of God with the collective voice of the praying community.

Benedictus es, Domine

Benedictus es, Domine" is a brief acclamation that is often included in the liturgy, especially during Morning Prayer. The Latin phrase translates to "Blessed are You, O Lord." It serves as a moment of focused praise and adoration, recognizing the holiness and blessedness of God. Here's a representation of how it might be structured:

Leader (L): Benedictus es, Domine.

All (A): Blessed are You, O Lord.

This simple acclamation is a direct expression of praise and acknowledgment of God's blessedness. It punctuates the prayer, providing a moment of reverence and collective affirmation within the worshiping community. While concise, it holds significant meaning, emphasizing the divine attributes and inviting the participants to join in the proclamation of God's blessed nature.

Intercessions

Intercessions in Morning Prayer offer a communal opportunity to bring forth petitions and prayers for the needs of the Church, the world, and individuals. The intercessory prayers express the unity of the praying community in lifting up concerns to God. Here is a representation of how intercessions might be structured:

Leader (L): In our morning prayer, let us turn to God, our loving Father, who hears the cries of His people.

All (A): Lord, hear our prayer.

L: For the Church, that it may be a beacon of hope and a source of inspiration for all seeking the path of righteousness.

A: Lord, hear our prayer.

L: For leaders of nations, that they may govern with wisdom, justice, and compassion, promoting peace and well-being for all.

A: Lord, hear our prayer.

L: For all those in need— the sick, the lonely, the oppressed— that they may find solace in God's love and the support of their communities.

A: Lord, hear our prayer.

L: For families and communities, that they may be places of love, understanding, and support.

A: Lord, hear our prayer.

L: For all who work for justice and peace, that their efforts may bear fruit in a world longing for harmony.

A: Lord, hear our prayer.

L: For the intentions we hold in the silence of our hearts.
(Pause for personal intentions.)

A: Lord, hear our prayer.

L: We entrust our prayers to the intercession of Mary, the Mother of God, and all the saints who have gone before us.

A: Hail Mary, full of grace, the Lord is with thee...

L: Let us pray.

A: Amen.

These intercessions allow the praying community to lift up various concerns and hopes, fostering a sense of collective responsibility and care. The response "Lord, hear our prayer" reflects the communal plea for God's guidance, mercy, and intervention in the various aspects of life. The inclusion of personal intentions and the closing prayer acknowledge the diversity of needs within the community and seek the intercession of Mary and the saints.

Lord's Prayer

The Lord's Prayer, also known as the Our Father, is a central prayer in Christian tradition and is often recited during Morning Prayer. It is a prayer that Jesus taught his disciples, and it holds deep significance in Christian worship. Here is a representation of how the Lord's Prayer might be recited during Morning Prayer:

Leader (L): Let us pray as Jesus taught us:

All (A): Our Father, who art in heaven, hallowed be Thy name; Thy kingdom come; Thy will be done on earth as it is in heaven. Give us this day our daily bread; and forgive us our trespasses, as we forgive those who trespass against us; and lead us not into temptation, but deliver us from evil. Amen.

The Lord's Prayer is a profound and universal expression of faith, acknowledging God's holiness, seeking His guidance and provision, and expressing the desire for forgiveness and deliverance from temptation. It serves as a unifying prayer that transcends denominational boundaries, bringing believers together in a shared expression of devotion and dependence on God.

Concluding prayer

The concluding prayer in Morning Prayer serves as a summarizing petition, asking for God's blessings and guidance for the day ahead. It is a moment of closure, expressing gratitude and seeking divine assistance. Here is a representation of how a concluding prayer might be structured:

Leader (L): Let us pray.

All (A): Amen.

L: Lord God, source of light and truth, as we conclude our morning prayer, we entrust this new day to your loving care. May your wisdom guide our steps, your grace strengthen our hearts, and your peace dwell within us. Bless us with the awareness of your presence throughout this day, that in all we say and do, we may glorify you. We ask this through Christ our Lord.

A: Amen.

The concluding prayer acknowledges God's role as the source of light and truth, seeks guidance and strength for the day, and expresses a desire to live in accordance with God's will. The "Amen" serves as a collective affirmation of the prayer, signifying the unity of the praying community in concluding the morning liturgy.

4

Midday Prayer (Sext)

Midday Prayer, also known as Sext in the traditional Christian liturgy, is a sacred pause in the day, providing a moment for reflection, renewal, and connection with the divine. As the sun reaches its zenith, Midday Prayer invites individuals to interrupt their daily activities and turn their hearts and minds to God. This prayerful interlude serves as a spiritual oasis, offering a brief respite from the demands of the day and an opportunity to realign with the sacred.

The opening invocations for Midday Prayer set the tone for this sacred pause in the day, inviting individuals to turn their hearts toward the divine. Here's a representation of how the opening invocations might be structured:

Leader (L): In the name of the Father, and of the Son, and of the Holy Spirit.

All (A): Amen.

L: O God, come to our assistance.

A: Lord, make haste to help us.

L: Glory to the Father, and to the Son, and to the Holy Spirit.

A: As it was in the beginning, is now, and will be forever. Amen.

These opening invocations establish a sacred rhythm, calling upon the Holy Trinity and invoking the presence of God. The call for assistance and help recognizes human dependence on the divine, fostering a sense of humility and openness to God's guidance. The declaration of glory acknowledges the eternal nature of God and the continuity of worship throughout time. This brief sequence of invocations creates a contemplative space, preparing individuals to enter into the Midday Prayer with reverence and attentiveness.

Scripture reading

A scripture reading during Midday Prayer provides a moment for contemplation and reflection on the Word of God. Here's an example:

Leader (L): A reading from the Book of Isaiah.

All (A): Thanks be to God.

L: "For I am about to create new heavens and a new earth; the former things shall not be remembered or come to mind. But be glad and rejoice forever in what I am creating; for I am about to create Jerusalem as a joy, and its people as a delight. I will rejoice in Jerusalem, and delight in my people; no more shall the sound of weeping be heard in it, or the cry of distress."

A: The Word of the Lord.

L: Thanks be to God.

This scripture reading from Isaiah conveys a message of hope and renewal, inviting those in prayer to contemplate the promise of God creating a new reality characterized by joy and delight. The "Thanks be to God" responses express gratitude for the Word shared during this sacred pause.

The responsory during Midday Prayer is a short, often antiphonal, response that connects the scripture reading to the psalms and emphasizes the community's response to God's Word. Here's an example:

Leader (L): The Word of the Lord.

All (A): Thanks be to God.

L: I am about to create new heavens and a new earth.

A: Thanks be to God.

In this responsory, the community responds with gratitude, acknowledging the transformative promise found in the scripture reading. It serves as a moment of contemplation and affirmation, linking the Word of God to the collective voice of the praying community during Midday Prayer.

Canticle

A canticle during Midday Prayer adds a lyrical and reflective element to the liturgy. One commonly used canticle is the "Benedictus," also known as the Song of Zechariah from the Gospel of Luke (Luke 1:68-79). Here's an example:

Leader (L): Blessed be the Lord, the God of Israel; he has come to his people and set them free.

All (A): He has raised up for us a mighty Savior, born of the house of his servant David.

Through his holy prophets, he promised of old that he would save us from our enemies, from the hands of all who hate us.

A: Blessed be the Lord, the God of Israel; he has come to his people and set them free.

1. He promised to show mercy to our fathers and to remember his holy covenant.
2. This was the oath he swore to our father Abraham: to set

us free from the hands of our enemies.

A: Blessed be the Lord, the God of Israel; he has come to his people and set them free.

1. Free to worship him without fear, holy and righteous in his sight all the days of our life.
2. You, my child, shall be called the prophet of the Most High; for you will go before the Lord to prepare his way.

A: Blessed be the Lord, the God of Israel; he has come to his people and set them free.

1. To give his people knowledge of salvation by the forgiveness of their sins.
2. In the tender compassion of our God, the dawn from on high shall break upon us.
3. To shine on those who dwell in darkness and the shadow of death, and to guide our feet into the way of peace.

A: Blessed be the Lord, the God of Israel; he has come to his people and set them free.

The "Benedictus" celebrates the fulfillment of God's promises through the coming of Jesus and emphasizes themes of salvation, forgiveness, and peace. It provides a moment for the praying community to reflect on the redemptive work of God in the midst of their day.

In Midday Prayer, intercessions offer an opportunity for the praying community to lift up specific needs, concerns, and gratitude to God. Here's an example:

Leader (L): Let us bring our prayers and petitions before our loving God.

All (A): Lord, hear our prayer.

1. For the Church, that it may be a beacon of light and love, sharing the message of hope with the world.

A: Lord, hear our prayer.

1. For leaders of nations, that they may govern with wisdom and compassion, seeking the well-being of all people.

A: Lord, hear our prayer.

1. For those who are burdened with illness or suffering, that they may find strength in your healing presence.

A: Lord, hear our prayer.

1. For families and communities, that they may be places of unity, understanding, and support.

A: Lord, hear our prayer.

1. For those working in challenging situations, that they may be guided by your grace and wisdom.

A: Lord, hear our prayer.

1. For the intentions we hold silently in our hearts.

MIDDAY PRAYER (SEXT)

(Pause for personal intentions.)

A: Lord, hear our prayer.

L: We entrust our prayers to the intercession of Mary, the Mother of God, and all the saints who have gone before us.

A: Hail Mary, full of grace, the Lord is with thee...

L: Let us pray.

A: Amen.

These intercessions cover a range of concerns, from the broader needs of the Church and world to personal intentions held silently. The "Hail Mary" and the concluding prayer express a desire for the intercession of Mary and the saints, acknowledging the communion of saints in the prayerful life of the Church.

Lord's Prayer

The Lord's Prayer, also known as the Our Father, is a central prayer in Christian tradition and is often recited during Midday Prayer. Here's an example:

Leader (L): Let us pray as Jesus taught us:

All (A): Our Father, who art in heaven, hallowed be Thy name; Thy kingdom come; Thy will be done on earth as it is in heaven. Give us this day our daily bread; and forgive us our trespasses, as we forgive those who trespass against us; and lead us not into temptation, but deliver us from evil. Amen.

The Lord's Prayer is a universal expression of faith, acknowledging God's holiness, seeking His guidance and provision, and expressing the desire for forgiveness and deliverance from temptation. It serves as a unifying prayer that brings believers together in a shared expression of devotion and dependence on God.

Concluding prayer

The concluding prayer in Midday Prayer serves as a summarizing petition, asking for God's blessings and guidance for the remainder of the day. Here's an example:

Leader (L): Let us pray.

All (A): Amen.

L: Gracious and merciful God, as we conclude this moment of prayer in the midst of our day, we entrust to you the hours that lie ahead. May the grace we have received sustain us, the wisdom of your Word guide us, and your peace dwell within us. Bless our efforts, guard us from all harm, and lead us in paths of righteousness. We ask this through Christ our Lord.

A: Amen.

This concluding prayer acknowledges God's grace and seeks divine guidance and protection for the remaining hours of the day. The "Amen" signifies the collective agreement of the praying community as they conclude their midday liturgy.

5

Evening Prayer (Vespers)

Evening Prayer, also known as Vespers in the Christian liturgical tradition, is a sacred time to reflect, offer gratitude, and seek God's presence as the day draws to a close. As the sun sets, this prayerful gathering provides a space for individuals and communities to pause, express thanks, and acknowledge the providence of God throughout the day.

Introduction:

In the quiet moments of approaching evening, we gather to lift our hearts in prayer. As daylight wanes and shadows lengthen, we turn our attention to the source of all light. Evening Prayer invites us to reflect on the events of the day, express gratitude for God's blessings, and seek solace in His comforting presence.

As we come together in this sacred pause, let us open our hearts to the peace that surpasses understanding. In the richness of this prayer, may we find moments of stillness, illumination, and communion with the Divine. Let us begin our Evening Prayer in the name of the Father, and of the Son, and of the Holy Spirit.

Antiphon:
   "O God, come to our assistance; O Lord, make haste to help us."

This antiphon serves as a call to prayer, recognizing our dependence on God's assistance and inviting His swift presence. It sets the contemplative tone for the Evening Prayer, signaling the beginning of this sacred moment.

Readings and Intercessions

Leader (L): A reading from the Book of Psalms.

All (A): Thanks be to God.

L: "The Lord is my light and my salvation; whom shall I fear? The Lord is the stronghold of my life; of whom shall I be afraid?"

A: The Word of the Lord.

L: Thanks be to God.

This reading from Psalms sets a contemplative tone for Evening Prayer, emphasizing trust and confidence in God as our light and salvation.

Intercessions:
   Leader (L): Let us bring our prayers and petitions before our

merciful God.

All (A): Lord, hear our prayer.

For the Church, that it may continue to be a beacon of light, guiding people to the source of all grace and mercy.
   A: Lord, hear our prayer.

For leaders of nations, that they may govern with wisdom and justice, seeking the well-being of all citizens.
   A: Lord, hear our prayer.

For those burdened by the challenges of life, that they may find solace in the comforting embrace of God's love.
   A: Lord, hear our prayer.

For families and communities, that they may be places of unity, understanding, and mutual support.
   A: Lord, hear our prayer.

For those who are lonely or feeling abandoned, that they may experience the companionship of the Holy Spirit.
   A: Lord, hear our prayer.

For all who are suffering, especially those affected by illness, poverty, or injustice, that they may find relief and healing.
   A: Lord, hear our prayer.

For the intentions we hold silently in our hearts.
   (Pause for personal intentions.)

A: Lord, hear our prayer.

L: We entrust our prayers to the intercession of Mary, the Mother of God, and all the saints who have gone before us.

A: Hail Mary, full of grace, the Lord is with thee...

L: Let us pray.

A: Amen.

These intercessions cover a range of concerns, from the broader needs of the Church and world to personal intentions held silently. The "Hail Mary" and the concluding prayer express a desire for the intercession of Mary and the saints, acknowledging the unity of believers in their prayerful journey.

Concluding prayer for Evening Prayer:

Leader (L): Let us pray.

All (A): Amen.

L: Gracious God, as we conclude this time of Evening Prayer, we thank you for the moments of grace we have shared. May the peace that surpasses all understanding guard our hearts and minds throughout the night. Guide us in your wisdom, strengthen us in your love, and grant us restful sleep. May our prayers rise like incense before you, and may your presence be a constant companion on our journey. We ask this through Christ our Lord.

A: Amen.

This concluding prayer expresses gratitude for the shared moments of prayer, seeks God's peace for the night, and requests divine guidance and strength for the journey ahead. The "Amen" signifies the collective agreement of the praying community as they conclude their evening liturgy.

6

Night Prayer (Compline)

Night Prayer, also known as Compline in certain Christian traditions, marks the final liturgical hour of the day. This sacred time, often observed just before retiring to rest, serves as a peaceful conclusion to the day's activities. Night Prayer provides individuals with a tranquil moment to surrender the events of the day into the hands of the Divine, seeking protection, rest, and the assurance of God's watchful presence during the silent hours of the night.

Antiphon: *"Guide us, waking, O Lord, and guard us, sleeping; that awake we may watch with Christ, and asleep we may rest in peace."*

This antiphon serves as a soothing refrain, a petition for guidance and protection during both waking and sleeping hours. It encapsulates the essence of Night Prayer—inviting the Divine to watch over and guide us through the night, ensuring our rest is embraced in the peace that surpasses understanding.

In the soft glow of candlelight or in the stillness of our hearts, let us commence Night Prayer, seeking the assurance that as we close our eyes to sleep, we rest securely in the palm of God's hands

Scripture reading and intercessions provide a moment for reflection and communal prayer.

Scripture Reading:
   Leader (L): A reading from the Book of Psalms.

All (A): Thanks be to God.

L: "In peace, I will both lie down and sleep; for you alone, O Lord, make me dwell in safety."

A: The Word of the Lord.

L: Thanks be to God.

This passage from the Psalms emphasizes the trust and peace that come from finding refuge in God, making it a fitting reading for Night Prayer.

Intercessions:
   Leader (L): Let us bring our prayers and petitions before our compassionate God.

All (A): Lord, hear our prayer.

For a peaceful night and restful sleep, that we may be renewed in body and spirit.
   A: Lord, hear our prayer.

For those who are anxious or burdened, that they may find solace and comfort in the loving embrace of God.

A: Lord, hear our prayer.

For those who are sick or suffering, that they may experience the healing presence of Christ in their moments of vulnerability.
A: Lord, hear our prayer.

For all who have died, that they may find eternal rest in the arms of God's mercy.
A: Lord, hear our prayer.

For peace in our hearts, our homes, and in the world, that the tranquility of God's love may prevail.
A: Lord, hear our prayer.

For the intentions we hold silently in our hearts.
(Pause for personal intentions.)

A: Lord, hear our prayer.

L: We entrust our prayers to the intercession of the Blessed Virgin Mary and all the saints who have gone before us.

A: Hail Mary, full of grace, the Lord is with thee...

L: Let us pray.

A: Amen.

These intercessions cover a range of concerns, offering a collective and individual expression of the community's needs, seeking God's guidance, comfort, and peace for the night. The

"Hail Mary" and the concluding prayer express a desire for the intercession of Mary and the saints, fostering a sense of unity and connection in the prayerful life of the Church.

Concluding prayer for Night Prayer:

Leader (L): Let us pray.

All (A): Amen.

L: Gracious God, as we conclude this time of Night Prayer, we thank you for the peace that surpasses understanding and the assurance of your watchful presence. May the night unfold its mysteries, and may our rest be guarded by your loving care. Grant us peaceful dreams and a renewed spirit as we await the dawn. Keep watch over us, O Lord, and lead us in the path of righteousness. We ask this through Christ our Lord.

A: Amen.

This concluding prayer acknowledges God's peace, seeks His watchful presence through the night, and expresses a desire for rest and renewal. The "Amen" signifies the collective agreement of the praying community as they conclude their nightly liturgy.

7

The Office of Readings

The Office of Readings, a distinctive part of the Liturgy of the Hours, invites individuals to engage in a deeper encounter with the Word of God. This prayerful observance, often associated with monastic traditions, provides an opportunity for meditation and reflection on scripture and other sacred texts. As we embark on the Office of Readings, we enter a contemplative space where the divine word becomes a guiding light, illuminating the path of our spiritual journey.

Introduction:

In the stillness before the dawn, we gather for the Office of Readings—a sacred time to immerse ourselves in the richness of God's word. As the world awakens, we turn our hearts to the timeless wisdom encapsulated in scripture, embracing the transformative power of the written word.

This prayerful observance transcends mere recitation; it beckons us to delve into the depths of divine revelation, to listen with the ear of the heart. The Office of Readings is an invitation to encounter God's word as a living, breathing entity—a force that shapes and molds our understanding, stirring the embers of contemplation within.

Antiphon: *"O God, come to our assistance; O Lord, make haste to help us."*

This antiphon serves as a melodic plea, a recognition of our need for divine assistance and guidance as we embark on the Office of Readings. It sets the tone for a prayerful dialogue, inviting the Holy Spirit to illumine the sacred texts and grant understanding to those who seek divine wisdom.

As we enter this contemplative space, let us open our hearts to the treasures concealed within the scriptures. In the quietude of this prayerful encounter, may the words on the page become a bridge between the human and the divine—a conduit through which the wisdom of God flows, shaping, and inspiring our journey of faith.

Office of Readings

In the Office of Readings, the selection of readings often includes passages from the Bible, the writings of the Church Fathers, saints, or other spiritually enriching texts. Here is an example with a reading from the Book of Isaiah:

First Reading:

Leader (L): A reading from the Book of Isaiah.

All (A): Thanks be to God.

L: "Do not fear, for I have redeemed you; I have called you by name, you are mine. When you pass through the waters, I will be with you; and through the rivers, they shall not overwhelm you; when you walk through fire you shall not be burned, and the flame shall not consume you."

A: The Word of the Lord.

L: Thanks be to God.

This reading from Isaiah provides reassurance and comfort, emphasizing God's presence and protection in times of trial.

Second Reading:

Leader (L): A reading from the writings of St. Augustine.

All (A): Thanks be to God.

L: "You have made us for yourself, O Lord, and our hearts are restless until they rest in you."

A: The Word of the Lord.

L: Thanks be to God.

This excerpt from St. Augustine highlights the deep longing within the human heart for union with God, encouraging contemplation on the source of true peace and fulfillment.

These readings are chosen to offer a blend of scriptural wisdom and insights from the rich tradition of Christian spirituality, creating a tapestry that guides individuals in reflection and prayer during the Office of Readings.

Responsory:
Leader (L): In the tender compassion of our God, the dawn from on high shall break upon us.

All (A): In the tender compassion of our God, the dawn from on high shall break upon us.

L: To shine on those who dwell in darkness and the shadow of death.

A: In the tender compassion of our God, the dawn from on high shall break upon us.

L: Glory to the Father, and to the Son, and to the Holy Spirit.

A: In the tender compassion of our God, the dawn from on high shall break upon us.

This responsory is a meditative response to the preceding reading, emphasizing the compassionate presence of God and the hope that accompanies it.

Intercessions:
Leader (L): Let us bring our prayers and petitions before our merciful God.

All (A): Lord, hear our prayer.

For the Church, that it may continue to be a beacon of light, proclaiming the message of salvation.
A: Lord, hear our prayer.

For all leaders and authorities, that they may govern with justice and seek the common good.
A: Lord, hear our prayer.

For those who are burdened by illness or suffering, that they may find comfort in the healing love of Christ.
A: Lord, hear our prayer.

For families and communities, that they may be places of peace, love, and mutual support.
A: Lord, hear our prayer.

For those who labor and toil, that their efforts may contribute to the well-being of all.
A: Lord, hear our prayer.

For the intentions we hold silently in our hearts.
(Pause for personal intentions.)

A: Lord, hear our prayer.

L: We entrust our prayers to the intercession of Mary, the Mother of God, and all the saints who have gone before us.

A: Hail Mary, full of grace, the Lord is with thee...

L: Let us pray.

A: Amen.

These intercessions cover a range of concerns, providing a collective and individual expression of the community's needs, seeking God's guidance, comfort, and grace during the Office of Readings. The "Hail Mary" and the concluding prayer express a desire for the intercession of Mary and the saints, fostering a sense of unity and connection in the prayerful life of the Church.

Concluding prayer for the Office of Readings:

Leader (L): Let us pray.

All (A): Amen.

L: Lord God, as we conclude this time of reflection and prayer in the Office of Readings, we thank you for the wisdom and grace imparted through your Word. May the seeds of truth sown in our hearts find fertile ground, bearing fruit in our lives. Grant us the strength to live according to your will, guided by the light of your Word. May the meditations of our hearts be pleasing in your sight. We ask this through Christ our Lord.

A: Amen.

This concluding prayer expresses gratitude for the insights gained during the Office of Readings and seeks divine guidance to live according to the wisdom found in God's Word. The "Amen" signifies the collective agreement of the praying community as they conclude their prayerful reflections.

8

Conclusion

Dear Reader,

Embark on a sacred journey through the "Pocket Guide to the Liturgy of the Hours," a profound companion that unveils the beauty and depth of this timeless prayer tradition. Within its pages, you'll discover not just a manual but a pathway to encountering the Divine in the rhythm of daily prayer.

As you delve into the intricacies of the Liturgy of the Hours, let this guide be your trusted companion—a beacon illuminating the richness of each prayer, each psalm, and each sacred moment. This is more than a routine; it's an invitation to weave the tapestry of your day with threads of devotion, offering a sacred cadence to your life.

In the midst of the ordinary, find the extraordinary. The Liturgy of the Hours isn't confined to the sacred spaces of a chapel; it breathes life into the mundane, transforming routine into a symphony of prayer. Your moments of morning praise, midday

CONCLUSION

reflection, and evening thanksgiving become a dialogue with the Divine, shaping your day into a sacred narrative.

Take courage, for this guide is your companion in establishing a prayerful rhythm. Embrace the structure it provides, allowing it to be a vessel for your intentions, reflections, and aspirations. In the liturgical tapestry, find threads of hope, joy, and solace intricately woven together—a testament to the universal prayer of the Church.

As you navigate the pages, may your heart be stirred with a profound sense of the sacred. Let the Psalms become your song, the readings your meditation, and the prayers your intimate conversation with the Creator. This guide is an entryway into the sanctity of time, beckoning you to participate in the eternal dialogue between God and His people.

May this journey through the Liturgy of the Hours be a source of renewal, a wellspring of grace, and a constant reminder that your life, every moment, is a liturgy—a divine symphony where you play a unique and irreplaceable note.

May your encounters with this guide deepen your connection with the Divine, enrich your daily existence, and become a source of profound spiritual nourishment.

In prayerful companionship,

[J. M. Gauthier]

Made in the USA
Coppell, TX
24 March 2025